# Goofus Glass

by
Carolyn McKinley

# Goofus Glass

by
Carolyn McKinley

COLLECTOR BOOKS
P.O. Box 3009
Paducah, KY 42001

The current values in this book should be used only as a guide. They are not intended to set prices, which vary from one section of the country to another. Auction prices as well as dealer prices vary greatly and are affected by condition as well as demand. Neither the Author nor the Publisher assumes responsibility for any losses that might be incurred as a result of consulting this guide.

Additional copies of this book may be ordered from:

COLLECTOR BOOKS
P.O. Box 3009
Paducah, Kentucky 42001

@$9.95 Add $1.00 for postage and handling.

Copyright: Carolyn McKinley, 1984
ISBN: 0-89145-251-6

This book or any part thereof may not be reproduced without the written consent of the Author and Publisher.

Printed by IMAGE GRAPHICS, Paducah, Kentucky

To my husband, Herschel McKinley, who has made me the envy of all my friends. His patience and encouragement made my constant search for Goofus a collectors dream come true. He is a special husband, good friend, advisor and critic.

# Acknowledgments

This book illustrating Goofus Glass is a solitary venture because the contents represent my collection with exception of four articles belonging to a good friend. However, as it progressed I realized this book could not have been done without the assistance of the following people who were so generous in contributing material which enabled me to arrive at a price for each article, and also valuable research material.

Charles "Buddy" Dodson, is a special friend who made my task both pleasant and possible. Without him, rare items of Goofus would not be illustrated in this book. He sold me most of his collection because he too wanted to share it. His knowledge of this rare old glass is outstanding, and his encouragement and generosity has meant much towards the completion of this book.

Everyone should have a friend like Jane Hand, another collector of this "ugly old stuff." Her constant interest and faith in my endeavor gave me courage many times. Jane has traveled many miles to purchase Goofus Glass for me, and when it was impossible for me to go she represented me. She has a great interest in this book and its contents.

The following people have been more than kind in assisting with the hunt. All listed below have always called and informed me where a rare old piece of Goofus could be found and on many occasions purchased it for me.

> Betty Gilmore
> Patty Heston
> Betty Helms
> Betty Null
> Gilbert Hutchinson
> Edna Odell
> Gerry & Carl Hawk
> Hatty & Harold DeHart

Last, but most important, thanks to my pgotographer and friend, Salvatore Patti, and my son, William Cranor McKinley. They tolerated my impatience and gave their expertise while excusing my anger and frustration when things did not - I thought - go well. Mr. Patti is highly skilled as a photographer and truly an artist with his camera. He did an excellent job displaying this glass as it is very difficult to photograph.

These people have my eternal gratitude for their assistance in helping me to bring some recognition to my "ugly old stuff." You are appreciated.

# Introduction

Carnival Glass, Mexican Ware, Bridal Glass, Pic Jars, Gypsy Glass, Hooligan Hooleys and Goofus Glass. These are some of the names this fascinating glass has been called since Harry Northwood started manufacturing it in 1897 and continued until 1910. It is not known just when the name Goofus began to monopolize the scene. The credibility of this unusual name goes to Earl Kittle whose wife is the author of the book *Early American Glass.*

The history of Goofus Glass is interesting and although it has been manufactured by several companies, it is believed that the Northwood Company with factories in Indiana, Pennsylvania, South Wheeling and Wheeling, West Virginia and Bridgeport, Ohio made the most. Many pieces bear their mark which is a circle around a large "N."

Goofus and I began our love affair years ago when I accidentally stumbled upon two Cabbage Rose vases. It does arouse your curiosity especially when antique dealers are so persistent in calling it that "ugly old stuff." So collectors, you are most welcome to the world of the most unusual poor man's glass there is - GOOFUS GLASS.

The reasoning behind the remarks "ugly old stuff" is that the beauty of the designs are almost obscured by the most obnoxious paint that is scaling off and this has cost Goofus it's rightful recognition. Only highly skilled technicians in mold design could have produced such detailed and articulate designs. These designs are found on large and small vases. They are roses, grapes, birds, butterflies, mums, poppies, but the most common and beautiful to me is the famous "Cabbage Rose." Also, these same designs are on bowls, plates, berry sets, saucers (and reportedly cups but this writer has never seen one), powder boxes, beautiful decanters, trays, water bottles and the most elegant oil lamps. These are not only clear glass but are found in milk glass, blue, green, amber opalescent, frosted, crystal and camphor.

There are many different ways you can enjoy Goofus. If the paint does not appeal to you, take a good paint remover and remove the paint and you will have a beautiful object because of the design. In most instances Goofus contains manganese which is a chemical used in the glass to make it clear and will cause the clear Goofus to turn a beautiful amethyst when exposed to the sun for several months. Another unique way to display your Goofus is to do your own painting. I have discovered that the beautiful shades of nail polish and a can of gold spray paint can make a thing of beauty. Use a little imagination and the results are most rewarding.

I have collected and read most everything written about this glass and it is the concensus of opinion that Goofus Glass pre-dates Carnival Glass but the two did share the limelight at fairs and carnivals. They were given as prizes but Goofus was left behind because the paint used on it was only sprayed on and not fired, therefore scaled off, but Carnival Glass retained it's finish.

So, who cares whether or not pickles were packed in this beautiful old glass it is so different, collecting is such fun and rewarding, and there are many who agree with me. Annette O'Connell of Redwood City, California has written one of the most outstanding articles on Goofus Glass Jars. I salute her for the assistance in helping to add some glory to this "Ugly Old Stuff."

# Pricing

The prices listed in this book represent the lowest to the highest price paid over a period of four years. Most of the Goofus Glass I have bought has been in and around Washington, D.C. and the metropolitan area, this represents the lowest price paid. The mid-west follows and the highest paid has been in the western states. This is attributed to the fact that the typical tourist collects and the market is good. Goofus Glass is found in flea markets and at auctions, and they all vary in price. Some pieces such as the decanters, powder boxes and plates are in great demand while the beautiful old vases are not. It is difficult to establish a good price guide for this old glass, so I have used my own and that of experienced Antique Dealers, also friends buying Goofus have been most helpful with this information.

An Antique Dealer will often price an article according to the condition that it is in. However, I have found them to be fair and knowledgeable in pricing. In the past two years more and more Goofus Glass is appearing in their shops which tells me that all my diligent searching and asking has not been in vain.

# Condition

The mint perfect piece of Goofus Glass is a rarity, but most collectors do not limit themselves to just these rare pieces. A true and conscientious Goofus Glass collector will see through the scaling old paint to the beautiful design and its potential.

If fortune smiles and you find a rare piece in mint condition, consider how fortunate you are but spice up your collection with a few which have not survived as well and show their age (and what a history is behind that age). Try your hand at painting, it is an experience. Look over the small chips and age cracks and consider just how old this beautiful glass is. Take it from me - IT IS CONTAGIOUS.

# Contents

| | |
|---|---|
| Introduction | 7 |
| Pricing | 8 |
| Condition | 8 |
| Vases | 10 |
| Lamps | 59 |
| Decanters & Water Bottles | 67 |
| Salt & Pepper Shakers | 73 |
| Syrup Pitchers | 76 |
| Powder Boxes | 78 |
| Trays & Miscellaneous | 81 |
| Milk Glass | 97 |
| Plates & Bowls | 102 |
| Bibliography | 128 |

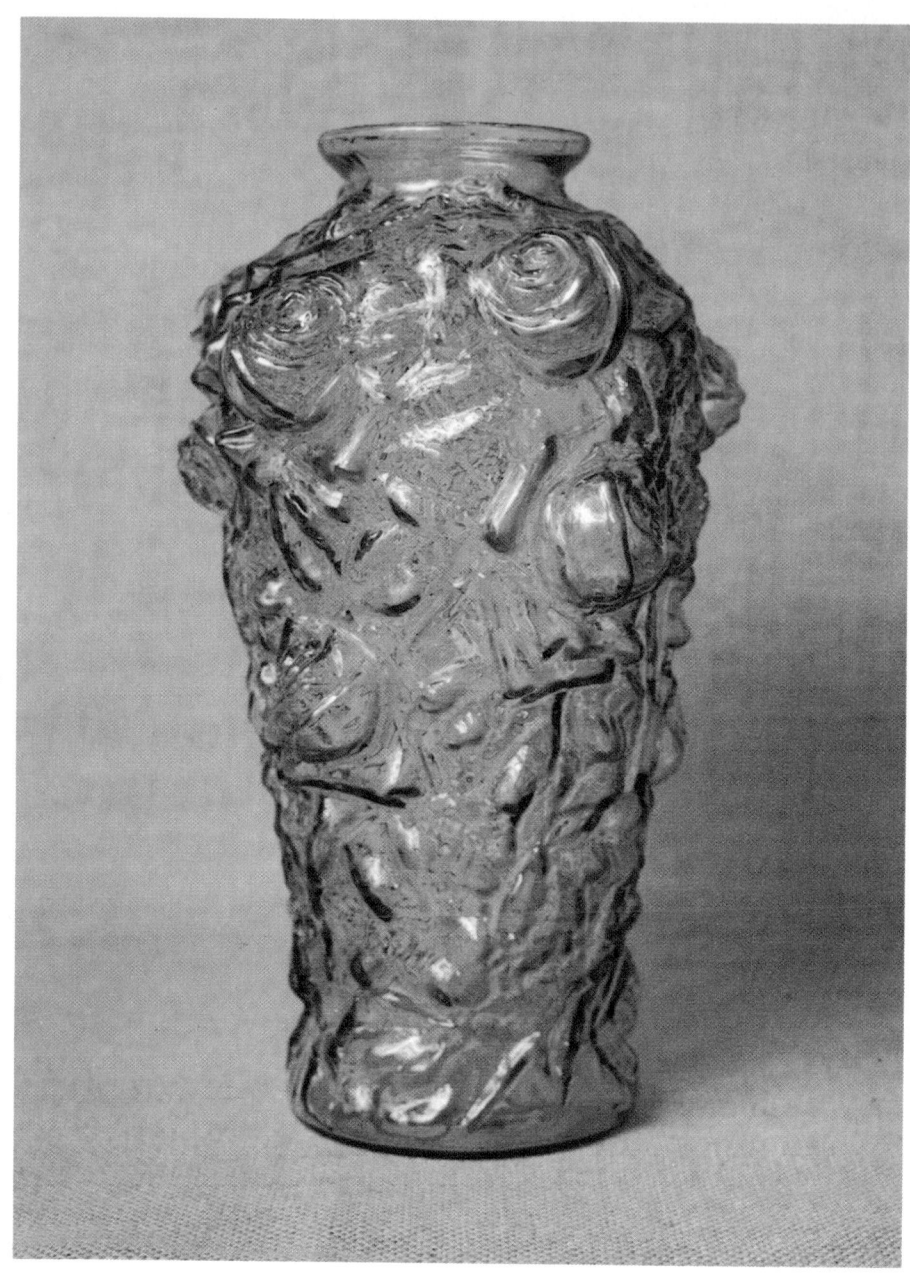

Cabbage Rose Vase or Jar. $50.00 - $60.00. 15″ h. This is one of the first jars off the assembly line. The paint was completely scaled off and it has turned the beautiful amethyst so lovely to watch happen. This is the largest jar I have found in the Cabbage Rose.

Cabbage Rose Vase or Jar. $35.00 - $40.00. 12″ h. Same vase only smaller. In the original paint. One of the few painted in silver. This also is one of the few in mint condition.

The Rose on Crackle Glass. $50.00 - $60.00. 14″ h. These are known best as Bridal Vases. They were given as gifts to brides. It is difficult to find crackle glass in the original paint. The vase on the right was painted by the author and the one on the left has turned amethyst. These are rare and very beautiful.

Grape Cluster on Crackle Glass. $50.00 - $60.00. 14" h. Same vase as the rose in size. The Grape Bridal Glass Jar is much more a rarity than the rose. The vase on the right was painted by the author and the one of the left has turned the beautiful amethyst.

A Flower on Crackle Glass. $50.00 - $60.00. 14″ h. Bridal Vase with the single flower and painted by the author.

Peacock In A Tree. $75.00 - $100.00. 15" h. A rare and mint perfect vase. In the front sits the Peacock in all its splendor and the back is only branches of the tree and flowers. The detail of this vase is both outstanding and beautiful.

Four Dogwood Blossoms. $50.00 - $55.00. 15″ h. The detail in this vase is most unusual as the blossoms are only on one side, the back is plain but it makes the flowers stand out. This was painted by the author.

Dogwood Blossoms and Hearts. $30.00 - $40.00. 15" h. An unusual vase in that there are six sides. The Dogwood Blossoms are in the front of the vase. The red hearts circle the vase only at the base, otherwise, the back is plain.

Three Chrysanthemums. $50.00 - $60.00. 15″ h. Three beautiful Mums only in the front of this vase. The mold design of this vase is unique and outstanding. Painted by the author.

The Peacock. $75.00 - $100.00. 10½ " h. The beautifully whimsical Peacock is displayed on this vase. The paint is scaling off but it is still a most unusual object just as is. This is a rare vase to find. Should it be found in the original paint the price would be more than quoted here.

A Cluster of Dogwood Blossoms. $50.00. 15″ h. This vase is identical in design to one in next photo only painted different. These are in original paint and in very good condition.

A cluster of Dogwood Blossoms. $50.00. 15″ h.

A Tree Rose. $35.00 - $50.00. 12" h. The vase on the right is in the original paint and mint condition ($50.00). The vase on the left is identical in design but the paint has scaled off, note the amethyst color ($35.00).

Four Poppies. $25.00 - $35.00. 12" h. In original paint and in very good condition.

Four Daisies. $35.00 - $40.00. 12" h. The interesting details on the side of this vase make it one of a kind. Small handles are in the mold design, the background is a basket weave design and very pretty. The flowers and leaves were painted by the author while the background is the original paint.

The Iris. $45.00 - $50.00. 12″ h. These three beautiful Irises are displayed only on the front of this vase. Another unique vase in color and design. The flowers are perfect but painted by the author while the background is the original paint.

Roses In The Snow. $10.00 - $20.00. 10″ h. This design is the most perfect rose on Goofus Glass. The beauty and quality of workmanship is expressed in this series. Painted by the author.

Grapes on Basketweave Design. $15.00 - $25.00. 10" h. The interesting detail of this vase is the shape. An hour-glass featuring grapes against a background of lattice work resembling a grape arbor.

The Regal Iris. $60.00 - $75.00. 10″ h. A very desirable piece of Goofus. Unlike many of the vases this one has two flowers front and back. It is a rare and beautiful vase and a favorite of collectors.

Three Mums. $55.00 - $60.00. 9½″ h. These three Chrysanthemums are displayed on a square vase making it one of the most unusual vases. The one on the right has been painted by the author while the one on the left is displayed in the original paint. They compliment each other.

A Matching Pair. $45.00. 9″ h. The vase on the right is an odd bird sitting on a grape vine while the other vase displays a ship at sea.

The Cabbage Rose and The Poppy. $30.00 - $35.00. (unpainted) 7″ h. Like the vase at the beginning of this book this vase is the smaller version. The Poppy is the same size, different design and is usually found together. The two here were the author's first two pieces of Goofus and are favorites.

The Cabbage Rose and The Poppy. $35.00 - $45.00. (Painted) 7″ h. The two displayed here are in the original paint. This is a matching pair which makes each rare.

The Six Sided Poppy. $15.00 - $17.00. 9″ h. A very common vase, its shape makes it attractive. These were painted by the author.

Grapes, Grapes, Grapes. $25.00 - $30.00. 10″ h. Six clusters of grapes decorate this rare vase, very thick glass slowly turning amethyst.

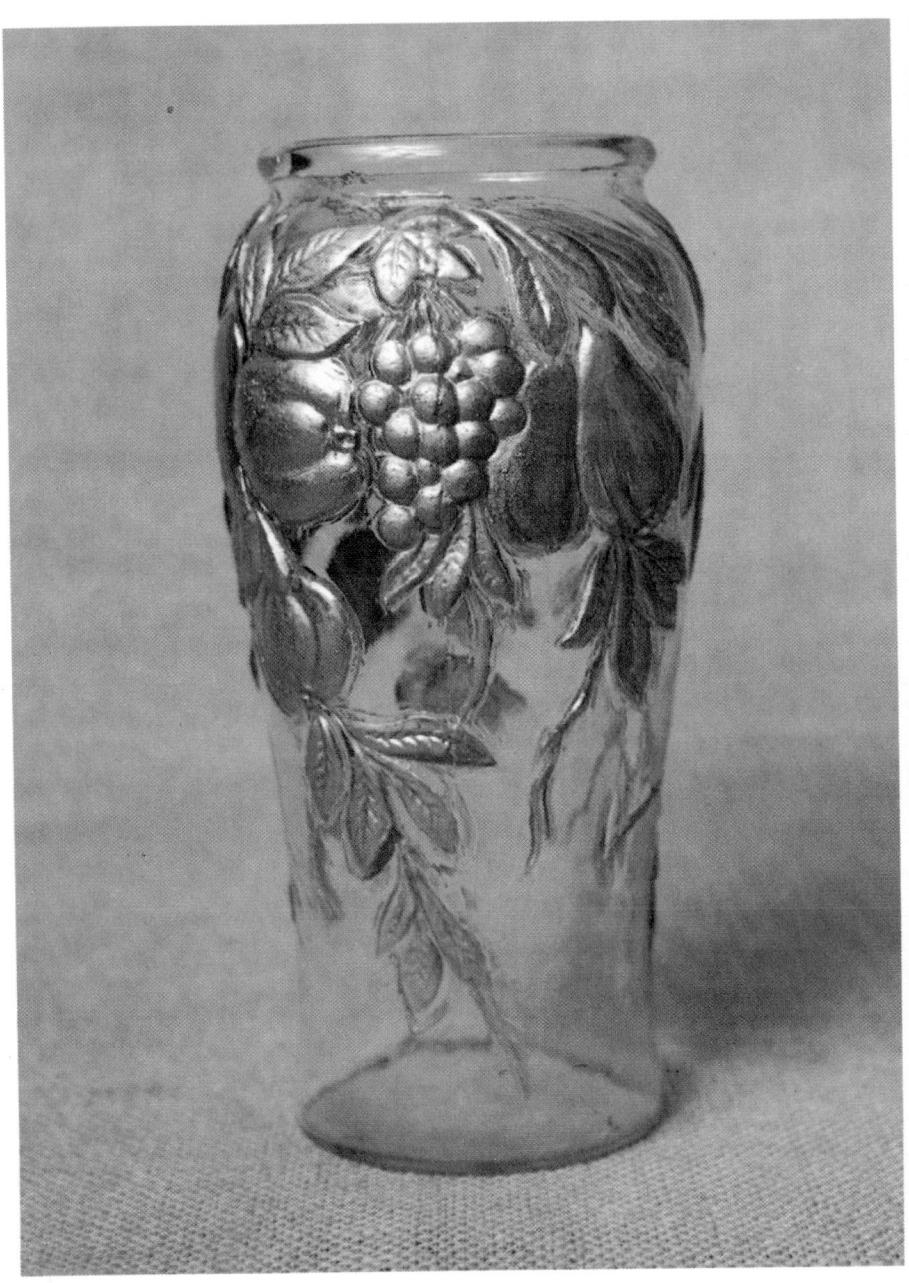

Mixed Fruit Vase. $35.00 - $40.00. 10″ h. A rare find in Goofus. The Indiana Glass Co. duplicated this vase in their Tiara Line. It was reproduced in amber color glass. This vase features pears, grapes and peaches. This is painted by the author.

Poppy Gone With The Wind Lamp Base. $50.00 - $60.00. 15" h. including the chimney. Without the globe this is still a beautiful lamp. It has turned amethyst and makes a unique piece with just a plain chimney.

Birds in a Dogwood Tree. $35.00 - $40.00. 10" h. This design is interesting-one bird in flight while the other one sits on a branch. Again this is thick glass but slowly turning amethyst. Painted by the author.

The Butterfly and The Poppy. $45.00 - $50.00. 13″ h. The Butterfly and The Poppy. $12.00 - $14.00. 3½″ h. These are very desirable vases and also very rare, the smaller one being the most difficult to find. They are very ornate but beautiful. The design is the same but their shape is so different one would have to look twice. This side shows a flying butterfly. Painted by the author.

The Butterfly and The Poppy. Same vase showing the opposite side which is a beautiful full blown Poppy. The same Poppy is also on the small vase.

The Purple Iris. $25.00 - $30.00. 10″ h. This vase has six complete stalks of the most perfect purple Iris. The gold background has scaled off and the vase has turned a beautiful amethyst. The flower has been restored by the author.

The Poppies. $20.00 - $25.00. 12" h. A rare shaped vase depicting two Poppies. The background has departed and the glass has turned that beautiful deep amethyst while the poppies have been painted by the author.

Three Clusters of Grapes, $15.00 - $20.00. 10″ h. Three perfect bunches of grapes with a lattice design between the grapes. Original paint.

The Perfect Flower - The Rose. $60.00 - $65.00. 9" h. The most elegant vase and one of the most challenging to restore. There are six perfect roses around the top and three larger ones around the bottom. The front shows the large rose and the back the stems and leaves in such a beautiful manner. This vase is truly a collectors item.

Back view of the Rose vase.

The Love Birds. $45.00 - $50.00. 10″ h. The Love Birds are only in the front of this vase but the back is as attractive as it is the continuing flower pattern and very attractive. This is a rare vase and this one has the original paint.

Bird Sitting on a Grape Vine. $10.00 - $15.00. 9″ h. Strange looking bird with a background of grapes. This vase is Satin Glass and painted by the author.

Grapes. $20.00 - $25.00. 7″ h. This is a rare vase depicting large bunches of grapes and vines. The rarity is the color of the glass which is blue and very thick and heavy glass. The paint has scaled off leaving this beautiful blue color.

The Squatty Cabbage Rose Vases. $15.00 - $20.00. 5½"h. The one on the right is the original paint and the one on the left has turned amethyst.

The Peach, Grape, and Rose on Crackle Glass. $10.00 each. 7½"h. These have shed the gold paint and have been restored by the author. They are favorites of many.

The Poppies. $25.00 - $35.00. 8½ " h. Beautifully shaped vase and unusual six large poppies and leaves. Restored by the author.

Rose Vase. $20.00 - $25.00. 9″ h. Showing roses all around the vase makes this one special, six roses in all.

The Poppy and The Rose on Basketweave Glass. $25.00 each. 10″ h. & 9″ h. These are very rare vases, different designs but both basketweave background. Restored by the artist.

The Single Rose. $25.00 - $30.00. 9½ " h. One of the most beautiful vases. Very thin glass with a single rose in front and one repeated in the back. Very special.

Morning Glory Vase. $25.00 - $30.00. 1½ ″ h. A beautiful vase with an unusual shape, partly restored by the author.

The Rose and Grape on Crackle Glass. $15.00 each. 9″ h. The Crackle Glass family presents these two straight vases, one painted, the other amethyst.

The Single Bunch of Grapes on Crackle Glass. $20.00 - $25.00. 9½″ h. A single bunch of grapes in front only displaying leaves. Partly restored by the author.

Four Chrysanthemums. $30.00 - $35.00. 8" h. An outstanding example of Goofus Glass. Displaying four perfect Chrysanthemums. Touched up by author.

The Wild Rose. $10.00 - $20.00. 10″ h. A beautiful vase with the wild rose blossoms all around the top of the vase also displaying leaves and vine, unique and beautiful.

Bird In A Berry Patch. $25.00 - $30.00. 10" h. The design is only on the front. A rare one. Restored by the author over the beautiful amethyst color.

The Grape & The Rose on Crackle Glass. $10.00 - $12.00. 6½ " h. The smaller version of these straight vases.

The Dogwood Blossom on Satin Glass. $7.00 - $9.00. 5½" h. A small vase on beautiful satin glass. The flower is front and back, small but very pretty.

Iris on Blue Glass. $25.00 - $30.00. 6½" h. An outstanding vase for it is small but very rare and unique in the style and color. Four irises surround this small vase. It is one of a kind. Partly restored by the author.

Goofus Gone With The Wind Lamp. $150.00 - $200.00. 17" h. One of the most beautiful and elegant oil lamps displaying the Poppy. In original paint. The chimney here has turned amethyst with age.

Goofus Umbrella Lamp with matching Decanter. $350.00 - $400.00. 19″ h. Elegant describes the lamp. In mint condition and very special to the author. Goofus La Belle Decanter with Stopper. $50.00 - $60.00. 9½″ h. This matching Decanter is also in mint condition. Original paint makes it very valuable and rare.

Goofus Fairy Lamp. $25.00 - $35.00. 7" h. This is an unusual piece, it is flash fired green. The perfect roses and shape make it unique. Three holes in the top are for the smoke from the candle.

Roses In The Snow Goofus Lamp. $75.00 - $100.00. 15″ h. including the chimney. This lamp with its glass base has been painted by the author but is very hard to find with the Goofus Chimney. So many ways to display these old lamps.

Goofus Cabbage Rose Lamp. $75.00 - $100.00. 15″ h. including the chimney. This lamp has turned the beautiful amethyst making it far too pretty to restore. Otherwise it is in mint condition, and very rare.

Dogwood Blossoms. $25.00 - $35.00. 10" h. An unusual vase as the top and bottom is frosted glass while the center where the blossoms are is clear. The vase has turned amethyst and is painted by the author.

Goofus Miniature Cabbage Rose Lamp with Chimney. With paint $40.00 - $45.00, without paint $30.00 - $35.00. 12" h. These lamps are very old but not too hard to find and they are lovely.

Tiny Miniature Goofus Lamp. - Blue Glass. $35.00 - $45.00. 9″ h. including the chimney. The color of this small lamp makes it very desirable to collectors.

Basketweave Water Bottle or Decanter. $35.00 - $50.00. 10″ h. An outstanding and rare piece. It displays a single rose on the front of the bottle with the same rose embossed on top of the stopper. In original paint.

Basketweave Water Bottle. $35.00 - $50.00. 10″ h. Another way the water bottle was displayed. Same bottle as in previous photo, only in white paint. The background is the original paint, the rose and leaves have been retouched.

Basketweave Water Bottle. $25.00 - $30.00. 10″ h. The same bottle again, paint has scaled off and turned amethyst, the rose and leaves have been retouched.

Grape Water Bottle on Crackle Glass. $35.00 - $50.00. 7½ " h. This is a very rare water bottle displaying the Goofus Grapes. A truly lovely piece.

La Belle Rose Decanter with stopper. $35.00 - $50.00. 9" h. This Decanter lost the original paint, it has turned amethyst and is shown here with a matching tray, too pretty to paint and a favorite piece of the author.

La Belle Rose Decanter with stopper. $35.00 - $50.00. 9" h. Same decanter and tray restored by the author.

Poppy Salt and Pepper Shakers. $25.00 - $35.00. 3″ h. In original paint turned amethyst with age. These are completely untouched. They are rare.

Dogwood Pattern Salt and Pepper Shakers. $35.00 - $40.00. 4″ h. In original paint wearing the original tops, these are also very rare and hard to find. Completely untouched.

Cabbage Rose Salt and Pepper Shakers. $35.00 - $40.00. 3½" h. In the original paint with the original tops but painted on milk glass. A rarity.

Poppy Blossom Salt and Pepper Shakers. $35.00 - $40.00. 3" h. In their original paint and tops. These are lovely and add to a collection.

Grape Sugar Shake on Milk Glass. $25.00 - $35.00. 4½ " h. This is a nice piece to add to your collection. In original paint and wearing its original top. Grapes front and back.

Strawberry Syrup Pitcher. $35.00 - $45.00. 6½″ h. In original paint and in mint condition. The top is missing.

Cabbage Rose Syrup Pitcher. $35.00 - $45.00. 5½″ h. The paint has scaled away but the color was too beautiful to retouch.

Basketweave Powder Box and Hair Receiver. $50.00 - $75.00 each. 3½ " h. Another of this series displaying a single rose on the side and the same rose on top. These boxes are seven sided. The Hair Receiver is on the right and the Powder Box on the left. The Hair Receiver is the most difficult to find.

Basketweave Powder Boxes. (Milk Glass) $45.00 - $50.00. (Plain) $25.00 - $30.00. Same Powder Box only in milk glass and very rare. In original paint and mint condition. The paint has scaled off the one on the right turned a beautiful amethyst. The rose has been retouched.

Basketweave Pin Tray and Jewel Box. (box) $45.00 - $50.00 (tray) $20.00 - $25.00 (box) 4" d. 2" h. (tray) 4½" d. Both pieces are rare and difficult to find. The Jewel Box is in original paint, the background on the tray has been touched up with the original paint on the rose.

Gibson Cameo Top Powder Box. $35.00 - $40.00. 3" h. 4" d. Love Birds Powder Box. $15.00 - $20.00. 3" h. 4½" d. Gibson Cameo Box has been retouched. It is rare and difficult to find. The Love Birds are satin glass, very attractive and have been retouched.

Puffy Rose Powder Box. $35.00 - $45.00. 3″ h. 5″ d. The larger of the Powder Boxes. The size and design make this piece most desirable. In original paint.

Puffy Rose Powder Box. $35.00 - $45.00. 3″ h. 5″ d. The same box only retouched and painted by the author.

Puffy Rose Powder Box. $35.00 - $45.00. 3" h. 4" d. Same as the Gibson Cameo only the top is Puffy Roses. This has been retouched.

Daisy and Plume Bowl. $45.00 - $60.00. 9" d. This opalescent bowl is standing on three short curved feet. The color is outstanding and in the original paint.

Wheel and Block Plate. $45.00 - $50.00. 9½ " d. This plate can be used for many things but it is mainly a collector's object. Original color and mint condition.

The Holly Plate. $45.00 - $50.00. 10½ " d. A beautiful opalescent plate in near mint condition in original paint.

Pinecones and Leaves. $45.00 - $50.00. 10″ d. A shallow bowl in mint condition and original paint.

Cabbage Rose Picture Frame. $35.00 - $45.00. 6½″ w. 10½″ l. The unusual blue glass makes this piece most impressive. This frame is holding a picture of the author's youngest granddaughter Jessica McKinley Hadlock - a very special piece.

Grape Tumbler and Footed Jelly Bowl. $35.00 - $40.00 each. Glass 4″ h., Jelly bowl 3″ h. These are very rare pieces on crackle glass. The tumbler is in original paint, on the grapes the gold has scaled off the rest and turned amethyst. The covered Jelly Bowl is footed and has a rose embossed on the top in gold, again the gold has scaled off this piece and it has turned amethyst.

Cherry Nut Dish. $35.00 - $40.00. 6½″ d. Unique and rare piece. Displaying a single handle and beautiful cherries in original paint. This is a flashed fired piece and it has retained most of the paint. The scalloped rim makes it a most attractive piece.

Flowered Coasters. $10.00 each. 3″ d. Set of four in the original paint, these are very rare.

"Last Supper" Bread Tray. $70.00 - $75.00. 7″ x 11″. This tray is common to find but the Goofus version is always painted gold, illustrated by the one on the right. The tray on the left has turned amethyst. The artistry of design is displayed here.

The Strawberry and Flower Pod Bon Bon Dish. $35.00 - $40.00. 4" d. These are sought after little dishes, dome footed and in original paint.

Rose Sauce Dish - Grape and Sunflower. $20.00 - $25.00. 5½" d. Dainty and beautiful dishes with the detail of crackle glass. In original paint.

Cabbage Rose Trays. (top) $25.00 - $30.00. 7" x 11". (bottom) $30.00 - $40.00. 5" x 7". These trays have turned the beautiful amethyst, they are painted gold with red roses. The large tray is common, the smaller one is more difficult to find. They are beautiful painted or unpainted and are the favorite of many collectors.

Basketweave Rose Tray. $25.00 - $30.00. 7" x 10". Very different from all dresser trays. The background of basketweave makes it unique. Touched up by the author.

Tulip Bowl and Field Flowers Footed Bowl. (Tulip) $20.00 - $25.00. 5½" d. (Field Flowers) $20.00 - $25.00. 5" d. These small bowls are different and in original paint. The Tulip is featuring scalloped rim and the Field Flowers serrated rim. These are both flash fired and very nice.

Poppy Card Holder and Poppy Relish Dish. (Card Holder) $15.00 - $20.00. 4" x 7". (Relish) $15.00 - $20.00. 4" x 7". These two pieces of Goofus Glass illustrate how versatile the mold technicians were. These are in their original paint.

The Rose Heart Shaped Dresser Tray. $50.00 - $55.00. 6″ w. 1½″ deep. This is a very rare piece. It has turned the beautiful amethyst and has been touched up by the author. A lovely tray.

Cabbage Rose Dresser Tray. $25.00 - $30.00. 6" d. This tray is also hard to find and beautiful to look at featuring 16 roses flash fired and in the original paint.

Fruit Tray. $100.00 - $125.00. 8½ " d. That mint perfect piece we all look for. All the fruit is painted with a flare that only Goofus has in original paint, a very impressive piece.

Hanging Grape Flower Pot. $20.00 - $25.00. 3″ d. 2½″ deep. This is for a very small flower but design is perfect. Unique piece in original paint turned amethyst.

Poppy Compote and Saucer in Crackle Glass. $20.00 -$25.00 set. 6″ d. 4″ high. In original paint and mint condition, this is a lovely set.

Goofus Perfume Bottle. $15.00 - $20.00. 3½" h. Only the paint on the flowers remains, but the pink tulips are many. This is a rare piece.

Green Poppy Plate. $20.00 - $30.00. 7" d. A signed Northwood piece, a large N with a circle around it in the bottom of this plate. In perfect paint.

Green Poppy Bowl. $20.00 - $25.00. 7″ d. 2½″ deep. A signed Northwood Piece (N). Shallow bowl in perfect paint and mint condition. Green Poppy Compote. $25.00 - $30.00. 6½″ d. 4″ deep. A rare piece and is signed. In perfect condition and original paint.

The Poppy Milk Glass. $20.00 - $30.00. 7″ h. The milk glass on these vases is very thick and the design as always is perfect. The paint has scaled away but it is still a collectors item. The Milk Glass Rose. $20.00 - $30.00. 7″ h. A most perfect rose is dislayed on this lovely piece of milk glass. No paint, but beautiful.

The Squatty Cabbage Rose Milk Glass. $20.00 - $30.00. 5½″h. Some prefer the milk glass painted but most enjoy it without paint, this is a much sought after vase.

Small Milk Glass Poppy. $15.00 - $20.00. 5″ h. A miniature Poppy vase without paint. It is rare. Small Milk Glass Cabbage Rose. $15.00 - $20.00. 5″ h. In perfect condition only minus paint.

The Dogwood Blossom Milk Glass. $15.00 - $17.00. 6" h. Unusual miniature vase in milk glass with only one blossom of Dogwood.

Rosebud in milk glass. $15.00 - $17.00. 6″ h. Same vase as one in previous photo, the back side is a rose bud in gold. Has been retouched by the author. Rare.

Cabbage Rose Miniature Oil Lamp. $50.00 - $55.00. 9" h. In milk glass this little lamp is most unusual, the design is perfect. It is special.

Carnation Cake Plate. $25.00 - $30.00. 12″ d. The gold has been restored on this hard to find plate.

Morning Glory Cake Plate. $25.00 - $35.00. 12″ d. Completely restored by the author.

Acorn and Leaf Cake Plate. $20.00 - $25.00. 12″ d. This is a beautiful plate without paint as it turned a beautiful amethyst. The gold scaled off leaving this fantastic design which has been partly restored.

The Carnation Cake Plate With Elk. $45.00 - $50.00. 13″ d. This is a very rare plate as it is in mint condition in original paint and the elk in the center is very life-like making the plate very valuable. Carnation Cake Plate. $20.00 - $25.00. 12″ d. In mint condition and in the original paint, this is a beautiful plate.

The Rose and Lattice Plate. $18.00 - $20.00. 6″ d. A small plate probably used to serve desert. The design is outstanding, this is the original paint.

The Rose Perfect on Crackle Glass. $18.00 - $20.00. 7″ d. This is the original paint and most unusual. The background goes from gold into a pale purple. The design of the rose on this small plate is perfect.

The Monk Drinking From a Tankard. $35.00 - $40.00. 7" d. In original paint and mint condition. This is a rare plate. The rose design around the edge is perfect.

The Cupid Plate. $35.00 - $40.00. 7″d. The two cupids in the center of this plate make it very valuable and unusual. The Poppy is around the edge and the plate is scalloped. The Cupid Shallow Bowl. $35.00 - $40.00. 6½″d. 1½″h. The bowl is on the left, still the same design. In original paint and in mint condition.

Goofus Plates. $30.00 - $40.00. 8½″d. This series of decorative plates is in perfect mint condition and in the original paint. These are The Roses and The Gibson Cameo.

The Grape plate and the Apple plate from the decorative plate series. (See bottom of page 108.)

The Single Rose. $20.00 - $25.00. 7" d. These matching plates are hard to find and are a collectors item. In original paint and mint condition. Plate "An Easter Opening". $20.00 - $25.00. 7" h. A chick coming out of an egg makes this plate unique and desirable.

Wild Rose Bowl. (left) $20.00 - $30.00. 9" d. 3" h. The gold paint has scaled off this beautiful set but the existing paint on the flower, leaves and stems is the original paint. Wild Rose Plate. (right) $25.00 - $30.00. 10½" d. Matches the bowl except the design is on crackel glass. Both have turned amethyst.

Strawberry Plate. (left) $35.00 - $40.00. 11" d. This is an unusual set in perfect paint and mint condition. Flash fired and turning amethyst. Strawberry Bowl. (right) $35.00 - $40.00. 9½" d. 4" h. Same as the plate with exception the amethyst is deeper in the bowl.

Iris Bowl. (left) $20.00 - $25.00. 7″ d. 3″ h. The regal Iris is displayed here in mint condition and in the original paint. This one is hard to find. Iris Plate. (right) $20.00 - $25.00. 8″ d. A true matching pair and the color is excellent in this set.

Grape Bowl. (left) $30.00 - $35.00. 7″ d. 3″ h. This is a very special set because it is difficult to find. It is indeed beautiful and these three pieces are in mint condition and the paint on them is excellent. Grape Cake Plate. (center) $45.00 - $50.00. 11″ d. In perfect paint. This series of grape design is one of the major motifs that Goofus Glass represents. Shallow Grape Bowl. (right) $30.00 - $35.00. 1½″ d. 2½″ h. A very important piece, the unusual shape makes it very valuable.

Roses In The Snow Bowl. (left) $10.00 - $20.00. 9″ d. In original paint and perfect condition. This series is quite popular and easy to come by. It is one of the most perfect Goofus Glass roses. Roses In The Snow Plate. (right) $10.00 - $20.00. 11″ d. This piece is in mint condition, the background has been retouched but the flowers are the original paint.

La Belle Cake Plate. (left). $35.00 - $45.00. 11″ d. This series of Goofus displays all the beauty, color and workmanship one expects from this glass. This plate is perfect and the paint is original. La Belle Bowl. (right) $35.00 - $45.00. 9″ d. This bowl matches the plate and is in excellent condition. The paint is original. La Belle Saucer. (center top) $10.00 - $15.00. 6″ d. Small saucer that fits a cup that has never been found. In perfect paint and condition. La Belle Berry Bowl. (center bottom) $10.00 - $12.00. 4½″ d. 2″ h. A small berry bowl in good condition. The background has been retouched.

The Dahlia Bowl. (left) $35.00 - $40.00. 10″ d. 2″ h. This set is very ornate in design as the flowers are so perfect. These are in excellent condition and mint paint. This shallow bowl is the rarest of the set. The Dahlia Cake Plate. (center) $35.00 - $40.00. 11″ d. Original paint and one of the best examples of Goofus Glass. The Dahlia Crimped Bowl. (right) $35.00 - $40.00. 9″ d. 3″ h. A smaller different bowl in shape. Perfect condition and original paint.

Five Sided Rose Bowl. $50.00 - $75.00. 9″ d. 3½″ h. Truly a monumental piece of Goofus Glass, very rare and very old. It is a round bowl yet the swirls make it have five sides. The paint has scaled off and only the roses have been restored by the author. The leaves are the original gold paint. It is a deep amethyst.

The Scalloped Dahlia Bowl. $45.00 - $50.00. 10" d. 4" h. Very ornate but beautiful. This is a large bowl perfectly scalloped which makes it most attractive. The gold has completely scaled off and it has been restored by the author.

The Square Grape Bowl. $50.00 - $75.00. 10" d. 5" h. This is one Goofus bowl that displays all the beauty and craftmanship ever displayed in glass. Scalloped yet square. This is the original paint, flash fired and turning amethyst.

Inside of Grape Bowl. Same bowl looking down inside. A beautiful piece.

Black Cherry Bowl. $35.00 - $40.00. 8" d. 3" h. Goofus was known for the odd sizes in bowls. Here is the cherry in another square bowl with rounded corners. Flash fired but wearing the original paint.

The Field Flowers. $35.00 - $40.00. 8″ d. 3½″ h. This scalloped and crimpled edged bowl is one of the most unusual examples. It is a small bowl and truly a collectors item. It is flash fired and has the original paint.

The Fruit Bowl. $25.00 - $35.00. 7" d. 4" h. A crimped bowl, flash fired with pears, cherries and plums. In original paint and very popular. Easy to find.

Cherry Compote. $75.00 - $100.00. 9½" d. 10" h. This compote is outstanding and beautiful. The cherry lined ruffled bowl is resting on a 10" glass pedestal, turning a beautiful amethyst. This is flash fired and the original paint. An example of excellence in design.

Goofus Grape and Cable. $35.00 - $40.00. 9″ d. 2″ h. This is the Goofus Glass version of The Grape and The Cable. The dome footed base stands the bowl up 4″. The gold has completely scaled off and it has been restored by the author.

Grape and Cable Compote. $25.00 - $35.00. 4″ d. 3″ h. This small compote is unique, a duplicate of the larger one in design and again the gold paint has scaled off and has been restored by the author.

Grape and Cable Candy Dish. $25.00 - $35.00. 5 1/4" d. 2" h. Another of this set turned amethyst, restored by the author.

Dogwood Bowl. $35.00 - $45.00. 9½" d. 3" h. Beautiful color and detail combined with the amethyst coloring make this bowl an outstanding piece to own. The gold is gone but the blossom and leaves are the original paint.

Fruit Berry Bowl. $35.00 - $45.00. 10″ d. 3″ h. ½″ thick. Beautifully detailed fruit bowl to a berry set. There are six small identical bowls. The glass on this bowl is ½″ thick, it is flash fired and the fruit is the original paint. A favorite piece.

Pinecones and Roses. $35.00 - $45.00. 9½" d. 2½" h. In full original paint this is indeed a thing of beauty, the eight sides with a painted rose between each panel tell it all. Artistry was not lacking in the days Goofus Glass was made.

Dogwood Blossom Bowl. $35.00 - $45.00. 10″ d. 3″ h. Ornate and in the original paint, this bowl stands out.

The Butterfly Bowl. $40.00 - $45.00. 8″ d. 4″ h. This piece is particularly desirable because it is figural, and in the original paint. It is flash fired and in perfect condition.

Roses In The Snow Bowl. $30.00 - $40.00. 9″ d. 2″ h. The bowl on the left was restored by the author while the one on the right is the original paint and in perfect condition. This beautifully painted bowl is resting on four glass legs and is a most desirable piece.

Grape and Lattice. (left) $35.00 - $40.00. 6½" d. 2" h. A nice example of the small bowls. The background has been restored but the grapes and leaves are the original paint. The Morning Glory Bowl. (right) $35.00 - $40.00. 6½" d. 2" h. This small bowl has been completely restored but speaks for itself that a little paint and imagination can make a thing of beauty.

The Rose and Lattice Bowl. $35.00 - $40.00. 7" d. 2" h. Small bowl with serrated rim, the perfect rose is featured here and in the original paint. The background of gold has been retouched.

Goofus Candy Dish. $50.00 - $55.00. 8½" d. 2½" h. Dome-footed with a figure eight around the inside and serrated rim makes this a most attractive piece. This is the original paint and it is in excellent condition.

La Belle Rose Square Bowl. $30.00 - $40.00. 5½" d. 2" h. La Belle design in a square bowl is different from any of the small bowls. Perfect and original paint.

# Bibliography

"Goofus Jars Mysterious," Hazel Geissler, Staff Writer. An article written for the St. Petersburg, Fla. Historical Society featuring the history of Goofus Glass and the collection of Mr. & Mrs. Clarence Wyman.

"Goofus Glass - Gorgeous or Garish," Ralph Bond - The National Bottle Gazette Volume 2 - Number 4 (1971)

"Goofus Glass Jars - Relic Hunt, USA," Annette O'Connell - Old Bottle Magazine
- Volume 15-Number 11 - November 1982